B.O.L.

B.O.L.T.O.P.

(Better On Lips Than On Paper)
The wartime love letters of Jim and Nellie Reynolds
1942-1945

Edited by Cheryl Mays

First published in 2024

Copyright © Neil Reynolds & Cheryl Mays 2024

All rights reserved

ISBN 9798324754402

Introduction

Jim Reynolds, from Eastleigh in Hampshire, was called up in July 1942 and joined the 23rd Hussars during the Second World War. 'Trooper' Reynolds became a Driver/Gunner of a Sherman Firefly tank during D-Day and the Normandy Campaign of 1944.

Nellie Moger, Jim's childhood sweetheart, worked at the Eastleigh Co-op as a grocery assistant, throughout the war years.

Jim and Nellie wrote over 700 love letters to each other throughout the war years and beyond. Remarkably, all these letters survive today, in pristine condition. They are full of humour, longing, anxiety and steadfastness during the most perilous and turbulent of times.

Jim and Nellie became engaged in 1943 and eventually married in 1947. Their love letters often ended with the abbreviation B.O.L.T.O.P. This wartime acronym was accompanied with many kisses at the bottom. B.O.L.T.O.P. therefore translated as 'Better On Lips Than On Paper.'

It has taken over 5 years to read and edit these wartime letters. What a privilege it has been. I have learned so much in the process, not only about wartime and the hardships and ordeals that many experienced, but also the resolve and faith of two young people caught up in a world at war.

This is their story.

Cheryl Mays, 2024

Private Jim Reynolds
Bodmin
Cornwall

July 5th 1942

Dear Nellie,
I arrived safely with around thirty other boys from Eastleigh. There was a sergeant at Bodmin to meet us. He made us march to the camp. It is a large place and the huts are warm and cosy. There is a big dining hall. It is twice the size of our Town Hall. We had a lovely meal of kidney mash, custard and apricots. On Friday we were inside with our kit, rifle, gas-mask and clothes. We have three suits of khaki, our walking-out kit, grey socks, gym clothes and towels. There is plenty of brass to polish. We have rifles to clean and boots too. There are lots of hills and valleys here. We are not allowed out though til Monday night because we have had our inoculations. Saturday night there was a concert, which was very good.

I wish you could have been here to see it with me. There is another one tonight and it is all free for the troops. Today for breakfast we had porridge and eggs. For dinner we had roast beef, potatoes and cabbage. All the food is good and plenty of it. We have coupons to buy cigarettes and one bar of chocolate a week.

There is a games room with easy chairs and a wireless. We are only here for six weeks and have to do three months training in that time, which is hard work. The beds are not very comfortable, just wooden bunks with straw mattresses. We have not had a siren here. I hope all is quiet in Eastleigh. Next week we do rifle training and marching, which I am not looking forward to.
Jim   XXX

Nellie Moger
33 Lawn Road
Eastleigh

July 7th 1942

Dear Jim,
I am glad to hear you arrived safely. I expect you were tired having to march all the way to the camp. It sounds as though you get fed alright, what with porridge and eggs. Talking of eggs, when your order went out on Friday, your family had omelettes! The delivery boy very carefully broke them, but I don't know how! The sirens don't worry you up there evidently. Today we had three in daylight, the first blowing at six this morning.

I thought I might go to Winchester on Wednesday to have some Polyfoto's taken. Then I could have some postcards printed off from the best.

Mum will be writing to you soon. At present, Dad is manicuring her feet with a razor-blade!
Nellie XXX

*Polyfotos-Multiple exposures were taken with a Polyfoto camera. The sitter was asked to look this way and that to catch a naturalistic pose

Bodmin

July 9th 1942

Dear Nellie,
Thank you for the very nice letter I had on Thursday. I could hardly wait to read it, but we had to go on parade. I am a little tired after all the marching. Today we went on the rifle range and fired live ammo. We each had five rounds and had a target to fire at. I got twenty points out of twenty five.

I went out of camp on Monday to have a look around the town. It is as big as Eastleigh and has a Woolworths and a Co-op. Also it has a YMCA, a NAAFI and a small picture palace. A railway line runs alongside the camp. When a train comes we shout "here comes the Bodmin Express!", and everyone laughs.

Well, the bugle has sounded so this is all for now, Nellie. Cheerio til next time.
Jim   XXX

*YMCA-The Young Men's Christian Association.
*NAAFI-The Navy, Army and Airforce Institutes.
The British government created the NAAFI to run recreational establishments for the British Armed Forces and to sell goods to servicemen and their families.

Eastleigh

July 11th 1942

Dear Jim,

It sounds as though you are getting on well with your rifle-shooting. Is it better than marching? And you don't seem to be starving on army rations, having eggs for breakfast every morning. No wonder we can't get any!

I went down to see your family on Wednesday and stopped for tea. Your mother said she was going to fetch Ernie and Pamela home this Saturday, as it is so desolate without them.

Your loving girlfriend,

Nellie XXX

Bodmin

July 12th 1942

Dear Nellie,

I am feeling alright now but was real groggy after my vaccinations.

On Wednesday we were on night operations, missing about four hours sleep. We went to a big range eight miles from camp. The weather was bad but we had a good shoot. We fired forty rounds each and also fired the Bren gun, which is easier than the rifle. We have to do Fire Watch here, although we don't get paid for it. We only have to get up if the siren goes off.

On Monday we had to run two miles in twenty minutes, with our full kit and rifle. I did it in nineteen minutes.

Our ramble on Sunday was lovely. We walked across fields and woods to a small seventeenth century church. Although it is miles from anywhere the Germans have tried to bomb it. There are three bomb craters in the churchyard.

*Bren gun- A light machine gun used in World War Two.

July 14th 1942

Today we were interviewed by the War Office, who are putting us all in the right jobs. I shall be a driver.

Listen to the wireless on Sunday, Nellie. They are broadcasting from the gym in our camp. Promise to listen in, won't you?
With love and kisses,
Jim XXX

Eastleigh

July 16th 1942

Dear Jim,

I hope you do pass as a driver. Your training will be up soon and then you will be due some leave. Did you remember your mother's birthday? Mother and I have sent a card.

I promise to listen to the wireless.

Ken Loveridge's sister is getting married on Saturday and Mum is waitressing.

Your loving girlfriend,

Nellie XXX

Bodmin

July 19th 1942

Dear Nellie,

This afternoon I went on a ramble to the ruins of Restormel Castle. We walked around the top and saw the old kitchen well and the pits where they used to throw the prisoners. The castle is perfectly round with a moat. From the top we could see Lostwithiel and Llanhydrock.

I hope you will forgive any spelling mistakes as I write this. I'm wearing my gas mask. We have to put it on for half an hour every Monday and Thursday.

One of the lads has just received his mouth organ. So we have a bit of music now. He can't play like Bill though.

Your loving boyfriend

Jim   XXX

Eastleigh

July 22nd 1942

Dear Jim,
I will forgive the mistakes you have made, but don't let it occur again! It must seem funny writing whilst wearing your gas mask.

Last night I went down to your house and Norman was very carefully sorting out the salvage from the cupboard, whilst your grannie was darning his socks for him.

Pamela and Ernie have come home at last. Ruthie has got 'The White Cliffs Of Dover' on her brain. All you can hear her sing is "and Jimmy will go to sleep in his own little room again." The other night she stood at the kitchen door and said "who wants a fight?" She had a piece of wood in her hand and told Bob to "stick 'em up" in her baby way.

*Paper salvage was launched by the British government in 1939 to encourage the recycling of materials to aid the war effort.

July 28th 1942

Yesterday morning we had the sirens go at six o'clock. The guns started soon after and of course, we had to get up. Your time is drawing to a close at Bodmin. You might be lucky and get posted nearer to Eastleigh. Let us hope so, Jim. We are thinking of all going up to London. I only wish you could come with us.
Your loving girlfriend,
Nellie   XXX

Bodmin

August 8th 1942

Dear Nellie,

It has been the hardest week since we have been here. On Monday we marched eight miles to the moors. We threw hand grenades, then had lunch.

On Tuesday we marched to Tregullan. On Wednesday we did some barbed wire fencing. On Thursday we did square-bashing and gym. On Friday we did a battle course. We went through bushes, a river and a tunnel. We were up to our necks in mud! After firing five rounds at a rifle range, we built sandbag walls and had a lecture on the anti-tank gun.

On Friday, at Tregullan, we heard a noise like thunder. Looking up, there were two Jerry planes, bombing and machine-gunning. So we had to lay flat under the trees. The bombs were dropped in the town, doing a fair bit of damage. Nine people were killed, eight from one household. The machine-gunner sprayed the camp with bullets and there are holes in our hut. Please do not say anything, or tell Mum, as she might get worried.

We leave here Tuesday, so there is lots of cleaning to do. We still don't know where we are going.

Your loving boyfriend,

Jim

XXX

*Square-bashing-A military drill performed on a barrack square.

*Bombing raid on Bodmin- "The Cornwall Blitz."

On August 7th 1942 two German Focke Wulf 190 aircraft dropped a succession of bombs and cannon fire over Bodmin Town, hitting the gasworks, a food depot and family homes. Eight people from the Sargent family were killed and their home wrecked. In total, nine people were killed and eighteen injured.

Eastleigh

August 15th 1942

Dear Jim,
Thank you for the brooch and photographs of Bodmin. Mother was dying to know what was in the parcel but she had to wait until I came home from work. So, you have moved to Durham! It must have been a long journey. I am glad you had your cake and bread pudding. I have received my Polyfotos. I will keep them here until you are home on leave. I am doing another bit of firewatch tomorrow.
With love and kisses,
Nellie   XXX

*Firewatch- In 1939 the British government were especially worried about the Luftwaffe dropping incendiary bombs. Stirrup pumps were distributed to local authorities and air-raid wardens arranged volunteer groups to help put out fires during bombing raids. Volunteers agreed to work on low pay after working in their normal jobs
during the day.

Trooper Reynolds
Barnard Castle
Co. Durham

August 19th 1942

Dear Nellie,
It was very nice to get a letter from you after eight days without any. I'm glad you liked the brooch. I went out Saturday to see Barnard Castle. It is much bigger than Bodmin. It has a Woolworths, a Co-op and plenty of pubs. I ended up in a museum in town with secret tunnels and dungeons. Oliver Cromwell was said to have hid here. You would have liked it.
We don't have rifles here, but pistols. These are a lot easier to drill with. I am now over three hundred miles from home, so a bit further than Bodmin! We have not started driving yet but will do so soon. We don't do firewatch here but do guard duty once a week. All day long we get gunfire. Rifles, pistols and big guns going off and it makes quite a noise. Also cars and tanks are moving about. I'm getting used to it now. Note my new address, Nellie. Also I'm not a Private anymore. I am a Trooper. The army must be doing me good. I have gained fourteen pounds! We pass out on September 16th and start our leave the next day.
Jim XXX

Eastleigh

August 21st 1942

Dear Jim,
Last week I went to the pictures with two girls from the shop. We saw 'Dumbo' in Technicolour. It was the story of an elephant with wings, who eventually gets taken on in a circus. We have had sirens down here nearly every day. Wednesday we had a day raid. The guns went off and the planes didn't half come over low. They took advantage of the low cloud. I believe Portsmouth had it. We brought four down, as far as I know.
Nellie   XXX

Barnard Castle

August 24th 1942

Dear Nellie,
Last night was moving night. We have now moved into a hut. We have to keep the floor polished and the windows clean. We have a wireless and electric lights. Today we were issued with rifles. We have been learning how to operate a wireless set and receive and send messages. I heard that there had been a raid on Bodmin Camp and that three new recruits have been killed. Lucky I am not there now.
Jim   XXX

Eastleigh

August 28th 1942

Dear Jim,

Down here the weather has improved very much. It has been too hot to work.

On Tuesday evening I went to the pictures to see "Blossoms in the Dust" with Greer Garson and Walter Pidgeon. It was so lovely. It was in Technicolour, and I wouldn't have minded watching it through again. Sirens are getting familiar again. Jerry is artful enough to get through in daytime now. This morning we had to go down the shelter. Mother has got a jar of Brylcreem here for you.

*Jerry- A nickname given to Germans during the Second World War.

September 7th 1942

Your leave is drawing close now, Jim. Only another ten days. Today has been a fine muck-up at work. Our Manager is going to live in Bournemouth. We have someone from the Romsey branch, but I don't think he is staying. Was my last letter to you censored, Jim? The letter I sent to a girlfriend was, but perhaps it is because she works in an aircraft factory.

Your loving girlfriend,
Nellie   XXX

Barnard Castle

September 10th 1942

Dear Nellie,

All this week we have been on gunnery, driving and mechanics. I think we shall be driving tomorrow. We have been issued licenses.

Last evening there was a sing-song in the NAAFI. Even the officers came.

I have not had any letters censored yet but some of the lads have.

Jim   XXX

Barnard Castle

September 25th 1942

(Back from leave)

Dearest Nellie,
Here I am, just arrived. I'm fed up and far from home. It is pouring with rain and very cold. I got to Waterloo alright and there was a lady in my compartment who was going to Darlington, to see her husband. I went by taxi with her to Kings Cross, so I saw a little bit of London. The train was packed and I had to stand nearly all the way.

September 27th 1942

The food here seems like muck compared to home! No eggs or bacon for breakfast. Not like last Sunday, and no lay in. Yesterday I went into Darlington. I wish you had been with me as there was a fair. I had a go on the shooting but never won anything. Got back to Barny at ten o'clock.
Your loving boyfriend,
Jim   XXX

Eastleigh

September 28th 1942

Dearest Jim,
I expect you were tired out by the time you reached your destination, having to stand all the way from Kings Cross to Barnard Castle!
Don't forget Jim, if you see a comb or a garden rake anywhere, get it and I will pay you for it. I am getting to the last tooth every time I use mine!
Last night I went down to your home and saw your family. They fed me up with custard tarts, walnuts and apples.

October 1st 1942

Sorry I haven't answered your letter before now, Jim. I have been to Southampton Road, to take the baby that I am nursemaid to, round to see your mother.
It is chilly down here and I have already gone into my winter woolies. Bill went to Winchester on Wednesday and got a game of Monopoly.
With love,
Nellie XXX

The very game Bill bought still exists.

Barnard Castle

October 2nd 1942

Dearest Nellie,
Nothing seems the same since I came back off leave, especially without you. All we had for tea yesterday was bread and jam and a little rock cake. The food here is like poison! I miss you as much as you miss me.
Next week we are driving cars all week and the following week we are driving Bren- gun carriers. Then we are learning the ins and outs of tanks, the big ones. Then we have six weeks of gunnery.
Tuesday night I had eight bars of chocolate from the NAAFI, which was due to me. I have sent some to you, dearest.

October 6th 1942

Yesterday we were harvesting all day, which was jolly good fun. Six of us went to a farm, in an army lorry. We got in the oats, which we had to stack in ricks. The gentleman farmer, being a nice bloke, took us to his house after. We had a hot dinner, a pint of ale each and a big slice of home-made plum tart.
Til next time,
Jim   XXX

Eastleigh

October 9th 1942

Dear Jim,
I expect it was fine fun harvesting and being in the open air. I was very pleased with the chocolate you sent. On Wednesday night we had three sirens and the 'double red' went for three minutes. The baby I take out is a sweet little thing. She has lovely blue eyes and is called Christine. I won a woolly rabbit in a raffle and gave it to her. She gets hold of the ears and chews away!
Nellie   XXX

*Air Raid Warning Sirens
'Double Red' was when all sirens sounded and you took immediate action and proceeded to a shelter.

Barnard Castle

October 11th 1942

Dearest Nellie,
Here is a good bit of news. On Friday I passed my driving test. This week I have to pass my Bren-gun carrier test. Tell Bill I am sorry I never sent him a birthday card. I completely forgot! I could not find you a comb in town but I am going to wangle one out of the stores, if I can.
Jim   XXX

P.S. What would you like for your birthday?

Eastleigh

October 13th 1942

Dearest Jim,
I hope you got the hot sweets. They should come in handy on guard duty. I can't tell you when I will get another tin from Boots, as Bill is thinking of leaving and going on a milk round at Hann's. Jerry is getting busy again. Today we had five sirens and Mum said that Brighton had it. I am thinking of buying a new dress. If it isn't asking too much, I would like some money as a birthday present, to go towards it.
Nellie   XXX

*Hann's Dairy- The dairy in Factory Road, Eastleigh, was the workplace of comedian Benny Hill and the inspiration for his hit record 'Ernie- the fastest milkman in the west.'

Barnard Castle

October 16th 1942

Dearest Nellie,

I've been on spud-bashing in the cookhouse. What a job! I worked nearly three hours. Are you getting any new marks on your envelopes? All ours now have a diamond mark. I'm wondering what it means?

A common sight up here are rainbows. Nearly every day I see one or two. I have seen more up here than I have ever seen at home.

Jim   XXX

Eastleigh

October 19th 1942

Dearest Jim,
Thursday afternoon your mother and your grannie came in the shop and bought three pounds of sultanas! So, watch out for your next cake!!
Nellie   XXX

Barnard Castle

October 22nd 1942

Dearest Nellie,
Today the camp had a visitor. The Princess Royal came to see the camp. I only saw her in the distance. She came in a posh car with a chauffeur.
Your loving boyfriend,
Jim   XXXXXXX
B.O.L.T.O.P.

*The Princess Royal – Princess Mary of York/Countess of Harewood (1897-1965). During World War Two, Princess Mary was Controller Commandant of the Auxiliary Territorial Service.

*B.O.L.T.O.P. - Wartime acronym for 'Better On Lips Than On Paper', referring to the crosses or 'kisses' written at the end of love letters.

Eastleigh

October 23rd 1942

Dear Jim,
On the bottom of your letter I see the initials B.O.L.T.O.P. Would you like to tell me what they stand for? You have beaten both me and Mother!
Nellie   XXX

Barnard Castle

October 27th 1942

Dearest Nellie,
B.O.L.T.O.P. means 'better on lips than on paper.' It is a new one that the lads have thought up.
Jim   XXX

Eastleigh

October 30th 1942

Dear Jim,
Wishing you many happy returns of the day! I do hope you enjoy the cake.
With love,
Nellie   XXXXXXX

B.O.L.T.O.P.

Barnard Castle

October 31st 1942

Dearest Nellie,

Many thanks for your lovely birthday card and present. I am sorry to say I am in hospital with a very bad chill. When the nurse took my temperature this morning it was still too high and the M.O. came and gave me some strong medicine. The ward here is a nice, clean place with six beds and a wireless. All the beds are full. I handed a piece of my birthday cake to each of the lads here and they were very pleased. The Eastleigh Weekly was very welcome in your parcel, as it is nice to read about what is going on at home.

I hope you will forgive the bad writing as it is awkward writing in bed. I have your photo on my table, next to my bed. You look nicer every time I look at you.

Cheerio,

Jim XXX

Eastleigh

November 3rd 1942

Darling Jim,

I am sorry to hear you have spent your birthday in hospital. Last week I went to the pictures and saw Don Ameche and Betty Grable in 'Moon Over Miami' in Technicolour, and it was lovely. Today at work we received an extra ten coupons for overalls. I have already spent mine.

Here's hoping you will soon be better and out of hospital.

Your loving girlfriend,

Nellie   XXX

B.O.L.T.O.P.

Barnard Castle

November 5th 1942

Dearest Nellie,

I came out of hospital yesterday afternoon and started work again today. I've been out on carriers all day, which is very tiring. It is very cold out over the moors. Last night I went to the sing-song. There was a guest artiste called the 'Fiddling Fool.' He had a violin and cracked a few good jokes. You would have rolled up with laughter if you had been here. There is only seven more weeks training now. I've been in the army eighteen weeks today. It seems more like eighteen years!

Your loving boyfriend,

Jim   XXX

B.O.L.T.O.P.

Eastleigh

November 7th 1942

Dearest Jim,
Did you hear about those three runaway trams at Southampton? They were without drivers and all of a sudden they went! A lorry driver with a load of sand managed to get in front of two and stopped them but the third one crashed. Someone said it might be sabotage.

November 23rd 1942

I went to the pictures last week and saw 'Weekend In Havana' with Carmen Miranda.
I have a new job at work now. I am on the bacon counter but it is messy and cold serving on marble. I have applied for the Assistant Cashier job, but I don't suppose I will get it.
Your loving girlfriend,
Nellie   XXX
B.O.L.T.O.P.

Barnard Castle

December 6th 1942

Darling Nellie,
This morning a Sargeant Major marched us over to the assault course. We all came through it but for a few cuts and bruises. I had a nasty gash on my leg.
We had to jump down five feet over a log wall, then climb a hundred foot cliff. Then we jumped a trench, then across a river and back again on ropes. We swung from a rope and fell onto some straw, then climbed through a tunnel. I did it all in five minutes and twenty seconds!
Jim XXX
B.O.L.T.O.P.

Eastleigh

December 7th 1942

Darling Jim,
I have been to Miss Willoughby's wedding reception on Saturday, so have not had much time for writing. It was a shock to hear about your Ernie the other day. He ran away, all the way to Portsmouth, by bus. I won't tell you anymore. No doubt your mother will give you the full details. Ernie was let off lightly though, not having a good hiding.
I have started knitting you a pullover. I am trying to get it done by Christmas and I am forfeiting my own coupons.
Nellie   XXX
B.O.L.T.O.P

Barnard Castle

December 13th 1942

Darling Nellie,

I have been to Darlington this afternoon. It was lovely, with all the decorations and lights. It was just like in peacetime. The streets were crowded with people and cars.

Jim XXX

B.O.L.T.O.P.

Eastleigh

December 15th 1942

Darling Jim,
I went to the Regal on Sunday and saw Reginald Foorte himself. Bill came with me and it was a jolly good programme, with Reggie at the organ. It did make a change.
Your loving girlfriend,
Nellie   XXX
B.O.L.T.O.P.

*Reginald Foorte- (1893-1980)
Reggie was a cinema and BBC theatre organist. He boosted wartime morale, travelling around England with a mobile organ, which he designed himself. He had a warm and personable style, combined with patriotism.

Barnard Castle

December 17th 1942

Dearest Nellie,
I am in hospital again, with a bad chill. We finish our training tomorrow. I do not want to be in here for Christmas. Last Friday we had to fire the Bren gun again. It poured of rain all day and we got soaked through.

December 19th 1942

I am a lot better and out of bed now. I hope to be out by Monday. I had my first Christmas cards today. There was one from Grannie at Twyford and one from Bill.
Your loving boyfriend,
Jim   XXX
B.O.L.T.O.P.

P.S. I still have your lovely photo on my bed table.

Eastleigh

December 22nd 1942

Darling Jim,
I am sorry to hear you have been in hospital again. Getting wet doesn't help, does it? That is how you caught this chill. I will not be able to finish your pullover by Christmas, but I am sending you a bottle of Brylcreem. I have only the sleeves to knit. I know it will fit you. I went down to your home last night and your father tried it on. I hope you don't mind him stretching it for you!
With love,
Nellie   XXX

Barnard Castle

December 22nd 1942

Darling Nellie,
I have now finished my training up here, thank goodness! I hope to be home next week.
I have sent you a little Christmas present.
Wishing you a very happy Christmas!

December 25th 1942

Today is Christmas Day. We had our Christmas dinner, which was served by the officers. The dining hall looked lovely, decorated with holly, flags and lights. We had roast turkey, pork, potatoes with gravy and sprouts. Then we had Christmas pudding with custard, mince pies and lots of beer. At tea-time we had slab cake and bread and butter. So that was my first Christmas in the army. I would sooner be with you, dear.
With love and kisses,
Jim XXX
B.O.L.T.O.P.

Eastleigh

December 28th 1942

Darling Jim,

I read your letter going up to London, in the luggage van. The train was packed. The van was empty except for a soldier and an airman, so I sat down on a bundle of blankets. I do hope you are lucky enough to get leave for the New Year. Coming home from London was terrible. We could only get in the guards van and that was full with people standing. It was so stuffy that three people fainted, so we had to open all the windows and turn off the lights.

I hope you have received that precious bottle of Brylcreem that I managed to scrounge for you?

Keep Smiling,

Nellie XXX

B.O.L.T.O.P.

23rd Hussars
B Squadron
Chippenham Camp
Ely
Cambridgeshire

January 10th 1943

(Back from leave)

Dearest Nellie,
Here I am, writing from my new address. It is four miles from the nearest village. The train took us to Ely. Then a lorry took us to this dump!
We have a little NAAFI in the camp and a nice YMCA. The food here seems pretty good.
Chin up, sweetheart,
Jim XXX

*23rd Hussars- A cavalry regiment of the British Army, raised during World War Two.
In existence from 1940-1946, it was assigned to the 29th Armoured Brigade of the 11th Armoured Division.

Eastleigh

January 12th 1943

Dearest Jim,

I can see by your address that you are out in the wilds. I expect it is lonely. Never mind. You are nearer to me now you have moved.

The postman knocked with your card.

Unfortunately there was only a penny stamp on it, so I had to pay him another!

I suppose you do feel fed up after being called back off leave. I see you are now in the Hussars. Isn't that a horse regiment?

From your loving sweetheart,
Nellie   XXX
B.O.L.T.O.P.

P.S. I have enclosed six stamps for you.

Chippenham Camp
Cambs

January 12th 1943

Darling Nellie,
There is no entertainment here and only one wireless in the NAAFI.
I have been blanco-ing our kit that dirty looking khaki green.
We don't have to walk into town. We have the 'passion wagon', which goes into Newmarket and brings us back again.
I hear they are going to make me a driver/mechanic. I will be given a tank.
Sunday afternoon I wore your pullover. It's lovely and warm and fits well.

*Blanco- Used by soldiers to clean and colour their equipment.

January 26th 1943

On Monday there was a big parade. We went in lorries and the tanks went too. They were lined up in a big field and every tank was flying a little flag. The King came at three o'clock. He went round standing up in a car. We all waved to him. He looked different in his army uniform.

January 31st 1943

On Thursday we went out driving tanks at the training ground. We lit a nice big camp fire and had our dinner there too.

On Friday at the YMCA, whilst writing a letter, a chap came up to me. He was one of the lads from Bodmin. It was grand seeing him again. He is not in the same regiment as me, but in the Lancers.

Jim   XXX

Eastleigh

February 2nd 1943

Dearest Jim,
On Saturday we had hailstones, storms, lightning and high winds. It brought four balloons down around Eastleigh including the 'Rec' balloon.
I am looking forward to your next leave.
Nellie XXX
B.O.L.T.O.P.

*Eastleigh had eight large barrage balloons during World War Two. They were used to defend ground targets against aircraft attack.

Chippenham Camp
Cambs

February 2nd 1943

Dearest Nellie,
Last night we had a concert in camp, given by 'C' Squadron. They sang 'When the lights of London shine again', and it made me imagine throwing aside the blackouts and the church bells ringing again. Every squadron has to put on a show and there is a barrel of beer for the best one.

My name was called out to go to the medical room for an inoculation. When I got there they told me it was the other Reynolds in our squadron, not me. The M.O. said another one wouldn't hurt me, so I had one buck-shee. This one is against Lockjaw.

With love,
Jim XXX

P.S. What does P.P.R.L.H. stand for on your envelope?

*Buck-shee - Free of charge.
*Lockjaw – When jaw muscles spasm and affect jaw movement.

Eastleigh

February 10th 1943

Dearest Jim,

I would like to thank you very much for the chocolate you have sent me.

Today we had a siren lasting one hour and twenty minutes. I expect you heard that Winchester had an unlucky packet yesterday.

P.P.R.L.H. stands for 'Postman, Postman, run like hell!'

Love,

Nellie   XXX

B.O.L.T.O.P.

P.S. Our little Ruthie was four years old today.

Chippenham

February 14th 1943

Dearest Nellie,

I hope you get to see that picture, 'The Day Will Dawn.' I saw it last Saturday in Newmarket.

That bit of Latin I wrote inside your envelope is our motto. It has been adapted from the motto written above the big gates, which lead into Chippenham Park.

'Dum Spero Spiro' means 'In Hope We Live.

Chippenham Park Gate

February 21st 1943

Yesterday I was on a fatigue all day and was dead tired when I got back. Eight of us moved twenty tonnes of steel. I can't tell you what it was for. For two days a week we are up at the tank training ground, driving tanks.

I have a good piece of news. I passed both of my tests and am now a full Gunner/Mechanic.

Thank your Mum for the lovely tarts. They were very nice.

Love,

Jim XXX

Eastleigh

March 5th 1943

Darling Jim,
I think your mother has a grudge against me lately. She has been in the shop twice this week and hasn't spoken to me.
Did you want some Germoline shaving soap? I will go to Wainwright's and see if they have any in.

March 8th 1943

I was on firewatch yesterday from seven o'clock. What a night it was too. At midnight the sirens blew. We went to the shelters as we didn't have any helmets. We thought we were in for it alright, but they passed over, dropping a few flares and incendiaries. The all-clear sounded around one thirty.
Nellie XXX

P.S. Now Jim, beat the band with this one : I.T.A.L.Y.

Chippenham

March 10th 1943

Dearest Nellie,

One of the officers has asked me to make a little bird table in front of his hut. I haven't got many tools, but I shall give it a go. It will keep me occupied. Some of the lads up here are making little gardens and painting their huts too.

March 11th 1943

Last night there was a free film show on in the camp. It was a very good picture called 'Mrs Miniver.'

I will try and do my best to get some leave at Easter.

Our gardens at the camp are improving. It doesn't half make a difference. Some have rustic arches and seats and lawns.

I can't understand Mum lately. If she still acts the same towards you, let me know. I will have something to say about it.

Your loving sweetheart,

Jim XXX

Eastleigh

March 19th 1943

Dearest Jim,
Your mum told me that she managed to get a stick of Germoline soap. At Winchester I bought six odd cups and a few chocolate biscuits.
Have you found out what I.T.A.L.Y stands for yet? I will tell you next time.
Nellie   XXX

Chippenham

March 26th 1943

Darling Nellie,

This weekend we are going out 'tramp-living', on what food we can find. We go out in pairs and have to make for a certain point. We can hitch-hike and leave camp on Friday morning. We must be back by Monday afternoon. I think this will be great fun.
I have found out what I.T.A.L.Y. means. I trust and love you.
Thank your mum for the lovely bread pudding.

April 4th 1943

Yesterday the weather was terrible. The wind was so strong that many trees were blown down all over the place. A great big tree came down right across the NAAFI.
What do you think we had for dinner today, darling? Egg and chips and rice pudding.
Yesterday a flying jeep flew over the tank park. It landed in the next field and taxied over to us. The pilot told us all about it. It was real interesting. He took off again and started stunting.
I did a little firing on the Besa gun yesterday. We fired tracer bullets too.

*Flying Jeep – The Hafner Rotabuggy

A British experimental aircraft with a rotor kite, developed to air-drop off-road vehicles.
*Besa gun – A tank-mounted machine gun.

April 21st 1943

I have been very busy these last few days, as I am now the Squadron Carpenter. I have made another bird table. This one has a thatched roof.
Good night darling,
Jim XXX
H.O.L.L.A.N.D. (Hope Our Love Lasts And Never Dies)

Chippenham

April 30th 1943

Dearest Nellie,
We have all been out on the moors again in our tanks, having mock battles. We had haversack rations for dinner. They only gave us a hard boiled egg each!

May 14th 1943

(Back from leave)

I arrived back at camp alright, about three o'clock. That parcel Mum sent had all gone bad.
About four o'clock some of us were detailed to go grenade-throwing. Then we were just in time for tea.

May 20th 1943

I am feeling very down-hearted because I have not heard from you. I hope you have received my last letter.
Last night there was a big raid near us, up here. It was very noisy.

June 3rd 1943

Since Tuesday morning we have been on a scheme. I have been riding on the lorry. Last night seven of us slept in this small truck. We had breakfast at five and nothing more til midnight!
We have got back to camp now.
We are on the move, so don't write any more just yet, dearest.
Jim   XXX

*Scheme – Army slang for Training Maneuvers.

Bridlington
Yorkshire

June 10th 1943

Dearest Nellie,

I have just arrived at our new billets. They are proper houses that the army have taken over.

We left Chippenham this morning and stopped a few times coming up. I was sorry to leave Chippenham as it was a nice place.

The town of Bridlington is a five minute walk from the house. There are plenty of amusements and I can see the sea from the end of the road.

June 13th 1943

I've been out to see the town again and it is a big place, with plenty of life and gaiety. There are six cinemas and the beach is lovely and sandy.

Bridlington has it's 'Wings for Victory' this week. All the flags are flying and the band plays twice a week on the prom. There is dancing in the evening too.

Jim   XXX

B.O.L.T.O.P.

*Wings for Victory – British National Savings campaigns during the Second World War, with the aim of Royal Air Force aircraft being sponsored by a civilian community.

Eastleigh

June 15th 1943

Dearest Jim,

Thank you for the view cards that you sent me of Bridlington. It does look like a nice seaside resort. It must feel like peacetime, sitting on the beach and enjoying the sea breeze.

Saturday night we all went to the fair, up at Oak Mount Road. It is here for three months for 'stay at home holidays.' We all had a ride on the roundabout and the bumper cars. What a treat!

Last Thursday night I went up to Red House, with the girls from work. We were learning how to put out fire bombs. We were there til ten thirty. You ought to have seen me, dear. I was in a pair of overalls, putting out a fire bomb on my hands and knees. Still, it was fun!

Nellie   XXX

B.O.L.T.O.P.

*Stay at home holidays – In 1942 the British Government encouraged people to holiday at home, within their local area. Transport networks were to be kept clear for troops and casualties. Local authorities aimed to provide outdoor entertainment and family-friendly activities such as fairs and county shows.

Bridlington

June 23rd 1943

Dearest Nellie,

All this week we have been receiving new tanks. The old ones are going tomorrow.

On Monday night I went to the Regal to see 'Random Harvest'. It was a real lovely picture.

Tomorrow I start on gunnery. More knowledge to keep in our noodle-boxes!

June 26th 1943

I am sitting on the beach, writing this letter. It is a lovely day with plenty of sunshine.

I'm on the new tanks again next week. They are better than the old ones but very slow. You can only do fifteen miles per hour. They weigh thirty tonnes.

Last night our troop were on fire picket again. We had to put out a real fire, which had started in a shed at about two in the morning.

We haven't had any sirens up here, just a few searchlights.

Our grand total of our 'Wings for Victory' week was £350. Well done, Bridlington!

Our troop officer was taken into hospital with a smashed face and the loss of a few teeth. He was in a tank and poked his head out of the driver's trap door and the gunner was traversing the gun. It hit him right in the face.

June 30th 1943

I walked down to the beach this afternoon and it was crowded with people playing in the sea, just like in peacetime. I met some of the lads down there and went in for a dip. It was nice and warm. We made a raft out of some petrol tins and old boards. We had some grand fun.
Later I walked to the Spa Theatre for an ENSA concert. I then went on to the Joyland Café and had a lovely supper.
Jim XXX
I.T.A.L.Y. (I Trust And Love You)

Bridlington

July 13th 1943

Dearest Nellie,

We have moved to a camp for a week, living under make-shift tents. It is fun living like this for a while, cooking our own food and making tea.

We are out on a big 'scheme' for four days. I have been driving the Squadron Leader about and today I even became the Commander. This was good fun as the tank was completely in my hands. I was giving orders all the time. One never knows when we may have to do this for real.

July 16th 1943

I am out on another 'scheme', on lorries. You get tired riding around all day. We have camouflaged up, waiting to move on again. We are back to our houses in Brid on Saturday, thank goodness.

You asked the difference between guard duty and fire picket. Well, the whole troop is on fire picket and we have to sleep in a separate house, with all the fire-fighting apparatus. If there is a fire, we all turn out to it. Guard duty is walking around, seeing that all is well.

I got a pay rise this week, so now I get twenty one shillings a week.

Today we are going to have a mock battle. Some infantry are going to attack us. We haven't got any live ammo, just blank rounds, that go off with a bang. It will be a bit of fun!

July 18th 1943

While we were out on a convoy all day, we had mock air raids, with planes going over, dropping dummy bombs. We were up at four in the morning, whilst you were still in dreamland, dear!

July 25th 1943

I received the parcel with the bread pudding in. I did enjoy it!
Jim   XXX

Eastleigh

August 4th 1943

Dearest Jim,

Bill has had his bicycle pinched at work. He told his foreman down the running sheds and reported it at the Police station, but no luck. It's such a drag for him now to get to work and back. Mum says that if it isn't returned, she hopes the bugger breaks his neck on it!

I was disappointed you not being able to get leave for Lilly and Fred's wedding, dear. It was a glorious day. I was Chief Bridesmaid and had to hold Lilly's bouquet when she got to the alter. We all enjoyed ourselves and went to bed at twelve thirty. The bride and groom went off to bed first and somebody had sewn their pyjamas up! Uncle Sid tied a tin of stones underneath their bed with a bit of string to pull, but it didn't rattle because the string broke!

T.T.F.N. (Tata for now)

Love and kisses,

Nellie   XXX

Bridlington

August 17th 1943

(Back from leave)

Dearest Nellie,
I got back safe and sound. It was a long journey though. When I got back to the house I found that the lads had been on a scheme.
I do feel lonely without you darling, but roll on next leave. What do you say?
Love,
Jim   XXX

Eastleigh

August 20th 1943

Dearest Jim,

I expect you have been downhearted since our parting. I missed you more than ever. We had such a lovely time together during your twelve days of leave.

After we left you on Monday, we stopped off at the Grantham Arms for a drink. The sirens went off and the guns started. We heard a plane had been shot down. We drank up quick!

Nellie   XXX

Bridlington

August 23rd 1943

Dearest Nellie,

So, Jerry had to come just as I left you Monday night! We have had nothing up here, just the drones of our planes going out. Let them knock ten bells out of them! There seem to be hundreds of them.

I went bathing again yesterday with the lads. It was lovely down there. We had some fun.

Friday night I went to the Regal and saw 'Casablanca.' Then the organ played 'Broadway Melody' and our favourite, 'Dearly Beloved.' Then we finished up with 'Land of Hope and Glory.'

I had a short letter from Lilly and Fred, thanking me for the wedding present.

Jim   XXX

Eastleigh

August 26th 1943

Darling Jim,

Jerry has been quiet since last Monday. I believe that plane came down on Hayling Island.

I weighed myself yesterday and now weigh seven stone and seven pounds. I have gained two pounds! If I go on like this you won't know me next time you come home on leave!

Nellie XXX

B.O.L.T.O.P.

Bridlington

August 29th 1943

Dearest Nellie,

Thursday afternoon we were all given new R.A.C. badges to wear on our tunics. I had the job of sewing on all the badges for the troop. I also have some carpentry work. I must repair the billets and houses.

Last weekend I volunteered to be a blood donor. The Red Cross took a pint of blood, then gave me a cup of tea and a sandwich and I got the rest of the day off.

I have received your parcel. The tarts were simply lovely!

Jim   XXX

B.O.L.T.O.P.

*R.A.C. – The Royal Armoured Corps

The Regiments of the Royal Armoured Corps form the British Army's Mounted Close Combat capability. Along with the Infantry, they are focused on close combat and destroying the enemy.

Eastleigh

August 31st 1943

Dearest Jim,

I was sent out to the Chandler's Ford branch again today. I don't know how long for. There are Canadian troops going through all day long, thousands of them. They are stationed nearby.

September 6th 1943

I am still out at Chandler's Ford and have been for over a week. I get the bus in the morning, take some sandwiches and come home around five. The Co-op pays for my bus fare. They are very short-staffed. I had a till all to myself til one o'clock, when a customer came in. The manager is much nicer than Mr. Chapman.

If you want anything knitted darling, I will willingly knit it for you. Can you get the coupons for the wool?

Love and kisses,
Nellie XXX

*Chandler's Ford had two camps during World War Two. They were for American and Canadian troops, preparing for the D-Day landings.

Bridlington

September 8th 1943

Dearest Nellie,

My mum and dad are coming up to Brid for a week, on September 18th. I thought you might like to come with them. What do you say? I will pay your train fare, so you needn't worry about that. We could have a lovely time as there is plenty to do.

We had last Friday afternoon off as a 'big knob' came round to see the regiment. We are having another day off soon, when the King comes.

And what good news about Italy giving in! Everybody is highly delighted and the lads said they were going out to celebrate.

Jim XXX

*The invasion of Sicily in July 1943 led to the collapse of the Fascist Italian regime and the fall of Mussolini, who was deposed and arrested on July 25th. The new government signed an armistice with the Allies on September 8th 1943.

Eastleigh

September 10th 1943

Dearest Jim,

I wrote a letter to Mr. Chapman, our Manager, to ask for the week off. He said he can't spare me. Could you write to Mr. Voss, the Area Manager? We can wait to see what he says. I don't mind paying my fare in the least, my beloved. As long as I can get the week off to be with you.

Mr. Voss has sent me to the Bishopstoke branch this week. It is nice and friendly here and only takes me ten minutes on my bicycle.

Little Ruthie has got whooping cough.

Nellie   XXX

B.O.L.T.O.P.

Bridlington

September 12th 1943

Dearest Nellie,

I am putting in for a day pass for next Sunday, dearest. Then we can have the whole day together. We might go to Flamborough and visit the lighthouse and caves, if the tide is out.

We managed to get two more cap badges. I am still waiting for the chain mail for the shoulders of my suit.

September 13th 1943

I have written to Mr. Voss, asking if you can have the week off. I shall be so disappointed if you can't come.

Fingers Crossed.

Jim XXX

B.O.L.T.O.P

The tailor's bill for Jim's dress uniform and chain mail.

Eastleigh

September 27th 1943

(After a week together in Bridlington)

Dearest Jim,
We arrived safely back in Eastleigh this evening. It was heartbreaking coming home and leaving you behind, my beloved.

October 7th 1943

Bill went chestnutting yesterday and got sixteen pounds worth! You don't eat them, do you darling? I had some grapes today at work. They were home-grown.
I am excited about our engagement, sweetheart. I hope you have written to my mum as you promised, darling. I can't wait for you to come home on leave!
Your fiancée,
Nellie   XXX
B.O.L.T.O.P.

Kirkcudbright
Scotland

November 11th 1943

Dearest Nellie,

I am now in Scotland! This could be for more than a month. I am at a farm, out in the wilds. We are sleeping in an old barn. The nearest town is about two miles away.

We have a little black mascot in our billet. It is a cat. He seems quite content here. I expect he wonders who I am.

I have now got the chain mail for my 'blues' and they do look nice.

I must wish you many happy returns of the day for your birthday.

Your ever-loving intended husband,

Jim   XXX

Jim in his "Blues" dress uniform with chain mail

Jim's son, Neil (centre), wearing the uniform at the Goodwood Revival

Eastleigh

November 14th 1943

Darling Jim,

I am wearing my ring to work and nearly everybody has seen it now. Our engagement is in the Eastleigh Weekly and my mother has sent you a copy.

I must thank you for my birthday card. What lovely words in it.

Nellie XXX

Scotland

November 15th 1943

Dearest Nellie,
On Saturday night I went into Kirkcudbright in the 'passion truck.' It is only a small village with a picture palace and a canteen.

We are about a quarter of a mile to the sea and there is a lighthouse quite near.

All day long we hear the tank guns from the different regiments, firing throughout the day.

There is only six of us Hussars up here. The rest of the regiment are back in Brid. There are about 500 of us here, all from different regiments.

Jim xxx

Eastleigh

November 18th 1943

Darling Jim,

It's not much fun for you without a wireless, is it, dear? I can't see how it is 'Bonnie Scotland' when they can't even supply you with a bit of music to cheer you up!

Now that you have your chain mail for your suit, do go and have your photo taken in it, when you get back to Brid.

Your mother didn't say anything about our engagement being in the paper. Ri and Eydy, from the shop, gave me a set of pillow slips for our engagement. That was nice of them, wasn't it, dear?

November 25th 1943

I have a terrible cold. Mrs. Dean, my workmate, has got the flu. Also two more staff have gone home with sickness. We shall have to shut the shop if this continues.

You have left one of your records at our house, Jim. Bill got out the gramophone and found George Formby's 'Auntie Maggie's Remedy.' I haven't told your mother we have it. Your mum was quite nice to me for a change last night. It was a shock to hear that your grannie had died. She never did get a piece of our engagement cake, after all.

Nellie   XXX

Scotland

November 25th 1943

Darling Nellie,
I have been busy making things today out of brass and metal. I have been cutting shell cases for the lads and making them into things. My hands are red raw.

November 29th 1943

I made a baby's cot for one of the lads, for his little nephew. He has just had a nasty bit of news. He had a telegram to say the baby had died. I told him he need not take the cot now, but he insists. I believe he is going on compassionate leave tomorrow.
I was very wild with my mum not sending for me for my grannie's funeral. I would have got leave. She said it would have cost me too much, but I could have got a warrant. I shall have more to say about it when I come home.
Jim   XXX
B.O.L.T.O.P.

Eastleigh

November 30th 1943

Darling Jim,

We are still four short at the shop, but Mrs. Dean came back yesterday. We worked overtime on Friday to get the orders out. The kiosk is closed at present. We have got a little heating in the shop now since the gas company came and put two new stoves in.

Your sister Gladys came in the shop this afternoon. She told me that she has given in her notice. She asked if they needed anyone in the shop. I told her to write to Mr. Voss.

Nellie   XXX

Bridlington

December 14th 1943

Dearest Nellie,
Here I am back in Brid. So far we haven't had any sirens up here.
I wish I was at home, spending Christmas with you, sweetheart. It would be nice, wouldn't it? This will be my second one away from home. A lot of the chaps are having their wives up here for Christmas. Lucky things.
I hope Ruthie is feeling better.
Goodnight, my beloved,
Jim   XXX

Eastleigh

December 17th 1943

Dearest Jim,

I went to the doctor's on Wednesday night, on account of my hair. He said I was to stop home from work for a few days. He gave me a prescription for some ointment. Mum has to rub it into my hair twice a day. The doctor says it is caused through the scurf in the hair. You wouldn't know me sweetheart. I look like an old witch!

Ruth is alright now. You can tell she is by the tricks she gets up to.

Mum and Bill are going up to London this Sunday, to take a set of saucepans up to the young man that Win knows, who is getting married at Christmas.

December 23rd 1943

Thank you very much for the Christmas card and the postal order, dearest. The money will come in handy as I am saving for a coat. I have sent you a bottle of Brylcreem and some razor blades.

The doctor says I have impetigo in the scalp. Mum had to wash my hair in antiseptic last night!

Mum and Bill had a nice time in London. I got my hand in here, acting as 'Mother' and cooking the dinner. Father pulled my leg over it but I took it all with a pinch of salt.

It is a good job kisses are not rationed or else we would have to ration our letter-writing, wouldn't we darling?
Wishing you a happy Christmas and a bright new year.
Nellie   XXXXXXX

Bridlington

December 26ᵗʰ 1943

Dearest Nellie,

Well, Christmas is over for us now. I had a really good time. On Christmas morning the Sargeant Major brought us all a nice cup of tea in bed. That was a first! Then we went to breakfast. Later we were all sat in the dining room for some great entertainment and a sing-song. At one o'clock the officers brought in our Christmas dinner. It was swell and there was plenty of beer too!

Jim   XXX

B.O.L.T.O.P.

Eastleigh

December 29th 1943

Dearest Jim,
It is a fortnight since I've been at work. My hair has improved wonderfully. I have had it washed every other day in Dettol and the stuff don't half smell!
You did make my mouth water, sweetheart, enclosing your Christmas menu. Now we know where all the turkeys went! We don't mind not having our share. After all, you lads deserve all you get and more.
Nellie   XXX

Bridlington

January 1st 1944

Dearest Nellie,
I must wish you a happy and prosperous new year! Last night I went to the Spa Ballroom. There was dancing and singing. I wish you could have been with me , darling. Just before twelve all the lights went out. Then the curtains went back on the stage and there was a huge clock. A chorus girl jumped right out of the middle. We all joined hands and sang 'Auld Lang Syne.'
Jim   XXX
B.O.L.T.O.P.

Bridlington

January 23rd 1944

(Back from leave)

Dearest Nellie,
Just to let you know that I have got back safely. There was a raid on at Kings Cross. What a noise! There were guns firing and bombs dropping and shrapnel dropping on the station roof. The sky did look pretty. I felt a bit jittery just the same.
I got back to my billet but the lads had all gone to Kirkcudbright. So I went to the canteen and then out to the pictures in town.
Lets hope the next ten weeks will fly by, til my next leave. It does seem a terribly long time though.
I lay on my bed this morning, thinking of everyone at home, especially you, my dearest. It nearly made me cry, coming back to this life again.
Jim   XXX

Eastleigh

January 26th 1944

Dearest Jim,

I was so anxious about you, knowing that London had it the night you went back. We had such a lovely ten days together, my darling.

I have picked up another cold since you left. I must have missed your warmth, my sweetheart.

You are to expect a parcel soon. My mother has sent you four Woman's World Libraries, a sponge cake and a tub of chocolate spread.

I went to the flicks last night with Bob and saw 'Arabian Nights' and 'Drums of the Congo.' Both films had spears and natives in and I'm not so fond of those sort of pictures.

I don't know how I stood on that station, to see you off, my sweetheart. I cried my eyes out when I got home.

On Friday we had a big raid and went down the shelter. Dad was at work and Mum was round the Meadowbank. We brought down twelve Jerrys. Both Portsmouth and Bournemouth had it though.

I got someone to weigh me at the shop yesterday. I now weigh 8 stone!

Our Rec balloon and the Barton Peveril one has now got lightning conductors on top.

January 30th 1944

We had another siren last night and brought down sixteen planes.
Last night I saw a man crossing the road, dressed in blues, with a yellow and navy cap and chain mail on his shoulders. I thought it was you. I'm not sure which regiment he was in though.
I am glad you like the chocolate spread. It does make a change from jam and lemon curd. Let me know when you run out, although it is scarce.
Nellie XXX

Eastleigh

February 4th 1944

Darling Jim,

Do you remember when we were walking up Twyford Road and we passed my fire watch mate? She didn't speak to you, but just stared at your chain mail. She told me that her father was in a horse regiment, in the last war. The chain mail was for cleaning the spurs and the horse harnesses. After he came out of the army, his wife used it to clean her pots and pans! You will know what to do with yours after the war, darling. Give them to me!
Nellie   XXX
B.O.L.T.O.P.

Bridlington

February 9th 1944

Dearest Nellie,

Yesterday morning we had a big parade, as General Montgomery was visiting. He spoke to us for about ten minutes. He is not as tall as I had thought and I stood within two yards of him. He is a very nice chap. He told us a lot of things that I can't tell anybody, although I would like to.

I have received the parcel safely. The bread pudding and sponge are most welcome.

Jim   XXX

Eastleigh

February 11th 1944

Dearest Jim,

Bill hasn't gone into work today. He is on the waiting list to go into Winchester Hospital. The doctor says he has a slow appendix.

Did you remember that little Ruthie was 5 years old yesterday? She had quite a few cards and money.

You remember when we went over to my cousins, that Sunday in Edward Avenue? The baby kept crying all the time. Well, they sent for Doctor Proverbs at 11 o'clock last night and they nearly lost the baby to bronchitis.

February 16th 1944

Uncle Jack came up last Sunday. He said he would make me an ironing board, when he can get the timber. This is for when we are married, dearest.

Two boys broke into our tobacco kiosk last Wednesday and stole two thousand cigarettes, valued at over ten pounds. Mrs. Kinsey had to go to court and give evidence.

Nellie XXX

Eastleigh

February 22nd 1944

Dear Jim,

We had a siren on Sunday night. It was all quiet by midnight. London had it again though. They hit Tate and Lyle's. We brought down five planes.

Did you know that your mother has not been well? Doctor Cheal has been treating her for 'Scabious.' However, Doctor Proverbs said it was no such thing. She had a rash all over for nearly a month. She was given a bottle of black medicine and a box of pink ointment, which she had to have rubbed in nightly.

While I was down at your home last Wednesday night, I had a glass of beetroot wine. Does that make your mouth water, sweetheart?

I went over to see my Auntie today. I am pleased to report that the baby is well again.

Nellie   XXX

B.O.L.T.O.P.

Bridlington

March 10th 1944

Dearest Nellie,

I have been swimming every day since Monday. It is real good. We have an instructor for an hour each day. If I can't swim by the end of a fortnight I don't think I ever shall! I am getting along well. We go to Hull in a lorry. There are two indoor pools and a big open air one. We use the indoor pool.

Jim   XXX

Eastleigh

March 14th 1944

Dearest Jim,

I hope you won't cut your fingers when you open this letter, as I am sending you a dozen razor blades!

On Saturday the Fire Service nearly flooded the High Street. They have built a pond on our bombed bit of ground. When they filled it up, one of the sides gave way. You ought to have seen the mess!

Nellie   XXX

Bridlington

March 15th 1944

Dearest Nellie,
I am still getting on well with the swimming. I can do three different strokes now. I have been nine times already. I stopped in Hull on Saturday, after swimming. I had some tea in an American milk bar. In Brid, the pier and the harbour have re-opened. There are no bands playing on the prom though.

March 23rd 1944

We had a big parade yesterday. The King and Queen and Princess Elizabeth visited us. They rode by very slowly in their car. I got a good view of them. It is the first time I have seen the Princess and doesn't she look lovely. She was dressed in a powder blue coat and hat. The Queen was smiling all the time.
Our letters are all going to be censored soon, so be prepared for missing words!
Jim XXX
B.O.L.T.O.P.

Eastleigh

March 26th 1944

Dearest Jim,

I hear that blue is one of Princess Elizabeth's favourite colours.

You gay old thing, going to the pictures three times in one week!

On fire watch last Friday night we had a siren lasting nearly two hours. The guns did rattle out. It was 1 o'clock when we got to bed.

I have another three razor blades for you. I got them in Winchester along with some biscuits, fruitcake and macaroni. So it was my lucky day!

Nellie XXX

Aldershot

April 20th 1944

(Back from leave)

Dearest Nellie,
Well, I got back safely to my new address last night, after leaving you.
I walked about a mile and a jeep picked me up and dropped me right outside the barrack gates!
I hope you got back safely.
I got the pot of jam and had some of the tart for supper.
Jim   XXX

Eastleigh

May 1st 1944

Dearest Jim,
Little Ruthie started school today. She likes it very much. She lost her packed lunch though but had her bottle of milk!
At the shop, Mr. Chapman has done nothing but shout at me this week. I can take it though, and give some back.

May 4th 1944

Win and I went to Winchester yesterday afternoon. We managed to get two pounds of macaroni. Have you run out of lemon curd yet, sweetheart? I have another jar here, waiting for you.
Bill has had his photo taken in his work clothes. He started work in Southampton today as a fireman.
How I long for the days to pass by now, knowing that I will see you at weekends, while you get the chance. It is nearly as good as having leave, isn't it, darling?
As I am a firewatcher, I must go to the Town Hall next week, for a demonstration of how to tackle a phosphorous bomb!
Your loving fiancée,
Nellie   XXX
B.O.L.T.O.P.

Brookwood
Surrey

May 12th 1944

Dearest Nellie,
I got back safely on Sunday night, but only just. A bomb dropped quite near. I expect you heard about it.
It has been raining all the time and it is rotten, especially being in tents.

May 30th 1944

We are not allowed out of the camp. I don't know when I will see you again, my beloved. Keep your chin up and keep smiling.
God bless you,
Jim   XXX

Eastleigh

June 9th 1944

Dearest Jim,
Goodness knows when we shall see each other again, now that this other business has started.
God bless you, sweetheart.
Nellie   XXX

*D-Day Landings- June 6th 1944. The largest seaborne invasion in history. The operation began the liberation of France and the rest of Western Europe, and laid the foundations of the Allied victory on the Western Front.

British Liberation Army
France

July 12th 1944

Dearest Nellie,

At last, here is my first letter to you, from somewhere in France.

I have not seen Ricky yet as he is fighting up at the front. One of my mates has gone back to Blighty. He was wounded but not too bad.

When we came across we brought six loaves of bread over and the lads here went mad for it! I managed to buy some potatoes and a bottle of coffee out here. We have to cook our own food. Tonight I am going to do some egg powder on toast. There are quite a few miles between us and a strip of water. How lonely it is now, sweetheart. You must be too.

We have been issued with plenty of cigarettes and chocolate. A chap bought my ciggies for a hundred francs. I am quite rich now!

The weather is good here. It is lovely and sunny but it makes everything so dusty.

Well, goodnight and god bless,

Jim   XXX

*A small number of tank crews of the 23rd Hussars were L.O.B., or left out of battle, under the command of 'B' Squadron's Captain Shebbeare. They were to be used as a reserve for casualties sustained in the initial battles. Jim Reynolds was part of this secondment and arrived in France just over five weeks after D-Day.

Eastleigh

July 14th 1944

Dear Jim,

I guessed that you were on the move. I know you haven't been in France long dearest, but don't forget to look around for a souvenir, because both Mum and I would like one, being as both of us have lost our handbags.

Your mum came in the shop yesterday and she had a letter from Ricky. He said he had been in action and had not seen you yet.

So, you are cooking and doing your own washing? I only wish I could come over and do it for you, dearest!

It is your mum's birthday tomorrow, darling. I could get a card for you, dearest? Would you like me to send you a tin of dried milk?

Glad Willoughby, from the shop, sent me a very dirty postcard! She is on her holiday. I have a good mind to enclose it with this letter, just to make you laugh.

Auntie Fan has been bombed out. Mum said she could stay with us.

We are getting raids every night now, with these 'jitterbugs'. They are terribly dangerous.

Keep smiling,

Nellie XXX

B.O.L.T.O.P.

*Jitterbugs; or Doodlebugs; The V1 flying 'buzz' bombs were launched against London and the South East of England from June 1944, by the Luftwaffe, killing over 6,000 people and injuring many more.

B.L.A.
France

July 17th 1944

Dear Nellie,

The church bells were ringing this morning. It did sound lovely and reminded me of home. I went to a church service at eleven.

We are digging trenches most days and moving on every day.

Yesterday I saw Ricky and the rest of the lads.

Jim   XXX

B.O.L.T.O.P.

Eastleigh

July 17th 1944

Dearest Jim,

I met your sister Gladys yesterday and we went for a walk down Magpie Alley. Afterwards we went back to your house for supper.

Your mum was making some blackcurrant jam and she gave me a jar to lick out. She told me she has made over forty pounds of jam from all the fruit in your garden!

I am on a fortnight's holiday from next week. I have no-one to spend it with and nowhere to go.

Glad tells me that someone else is taking over the Cosmo Café. Dorothy Shuffler is coming back as Manageress.

The jitterbugs are still doing the rounds. One dropped nearby last week, killing a baby and his grandpa.

Nellie   XXX

B.L.A.
France

July 19th 1944

Dearest Nellie,
I am still quite safe and sound, my dearest. It takes about a week for the mail to get to you, I think. It only takes two days to get here though.
I have seen all the lads and Ricky. I wish I was back with you, sweetheart. This horrible war has to be finished off, however.

July 23rd 1944

I wish I could be with you, sweetheart, in old England, instead of being up in the front line with Jerry. It isn't too pleasant out here, but we are back for a rest for a few days. It has been very trying.

July 24th 1944

There are hundreds of flies here and biting insects. They are similar to mosquitos and don't they bite! Our tea tonight was fried biscuits and sardines.
Jim   XXX
B.O.L.T.O.P.

B.L.A.

July 27th 1944

Dearest Nellie,
Last night I went to the pictures. It was in an old barn, with boxes for seats. The picture was 'Crazy House'. It took my mind off the war for a little while, although we could still hear the guns firing.

My watch has given up this week. On Sunday I took it off and dropped it in a tin of petrol. I'm lost without it.
I've just come across something I have never seen before. Mistletoe is growing on the trees over here. There is tons of it!
Jim   XXX

B.L.A.
France

August 6th 1944

Dearest Nellie,
Well, my sweetheart, here is something I can hardly find the words to say. My pal Ricky, was killed in action on Thursday. I didn't believe it when they told me. I have not seen his grave as it is up the front, along with five others that were killed the same morning. I feel rotten. I wonder what his wife will do now. He has a little girl too.
It was an '88' shell from one of the Jerry tiger tanks. It blew his head right off. Also Captain Shebbeare is missing from the last battle. No-one has heard a thing. He may be a prisoner of war.
I wish this horrible war will soon be over. We could be enjoying a lovely August Bank Holiday right now. Instead I'm sitting here writing this letter, with shells whizzing over my head all the time.
Jim   XXX

2004

Hero's return trip, Jim saying 'Goodbye' to Ricky after 60 years.

Ricky- Trooper Braithwaite Richardson, 23rd Hussars

Died August 3rd 1944 at Le Bas Perrier, France.

B.L.A.

August 11th 1944

Dear Nellie,
I went into Caen the other day to look around. There wasn't much there. I saw Caen Cathedral. It is a real mess. I also went to Cruelly. I went into a café and had my first cup of French coffee.
Jim   XXX

Eastleigh

August 11th 1944

Dear Jim,
It is sad to hear about Ricky. I expect you are upset, my darling. He was one of your best pals. I wonder if his wife has heard the news yet? It will be a shock to her. I hope you get news of your Captain soon.
Keep safe, darling,
Nellie   XXX

B.L.A.

August 16th 1944

Dearest Nellie,
Do you remember the day we first met, sweetheart? It hardly seems that it was 8 years ago. That was in the good old days, when we never cared two hoots about anything. How much has changed!
I hope it won't be long before we can all return to our loved ones.
We have a signals lorry near us today and they have a wireless. It is lovely hearing some of the old songs. It does remind me of home. I have heard 'I'm Riding For A Fall' and 'Shine On Harvest Moon'.
With love,
Jim   XXX

B.L.A.
France

August 27th 1944

Dearest Nellie,
We have been at this rest place for a few days now. I have been bathing every day. We have had some fun in the river, swimming and cooling off. I am sat by the river now, finishing your letter. I have been to an ENSA concert last night. There were three English girls, who sang and danced. They spoke to us lads afterwards too.

The other day we joined up with the yanks. We were glad to see each other. I have changed my opinion of them. They are a grand bunch of lads and worth fighting side by side with.

I had an apple yesterday, the first one I have had since being over here. There are plenty of cider apples, growing in the orchards. They are bitter and sharp to taste though. I found two trees laden with peaches yesterday. However, they were rock-hard and I was disappointed.

Jim   XXX

B.O.L.T.O.P.

B.L.A.
Belgium

September 5th 1944

Dearest Nellie,
The night before last, our lorry broke down in the middle of the town. We had just crossed the border into Belgium. We had a better welcome here than we ever did in France. Everybody cheered us with flags waving, like a never-ending carnival. The things we have been given! Flowers, fruit, wine and spirits. I have had more to drink than I've had in my whole life!

As I walked through the town, I couldn't move for people shaking hands. We were the first Tommys to walk through the town. It had only been liberated that morning.

We had to stay the night as the lorry couldn't be repaired. We were given a civvy bed in a posh hotel. The celebrations went on through the night. We had lots of kisses from local girls too. They didn't care if we were dirty! Don't get jealous, dearest!

Jim   XXX

Eastleigh

September 8th 1944

Dear Jim,

Mum went to London yesterday, to fetch Auntie Fan down to Eastleigh. When they reached the station, they had to jump from the train. It was too long for the platform! As luck would have it, there was a sailor who said he would catch her. So Auntie Fan fell into the arms of the Navy!

Mum brought us back an engagement gift from May and Ernie. It was a teapot cover and a case of green-handled tea-knives. That was very nice of them, wasn't it?

I hope you enjoyed your ENSA concert. I heard George Formby on the wireless the other night and he said he would be back in France in the next fortnight.

September 18th 1944

I managed to get a bottle of Brylcreem for you. Shall I send it on to you, sweetheart?

They have started sending the doodle-bugs over to London again. Poor old London.

Nellie   XXX

Eastleigh

September 20th 1944

Dearest Jim,

We all went to the hospital today to visit Bill. He has had his appendix operation. He didn't look at all well. Most of the hospital is taken over for soldiers.

Why didn't you tell me you were running out of ink, darling? I will send you some on, although I don't mind a letter written in pencil, dearest.

Nellie   XXX

B.O.L.T.O.P.

B.L.A.

September 20th 1944

Dearest Nellie,
I'm a little tired after being up all night. I have been driving all the way from Belgium into Holland. We crossed the border and the countryside is very flat.

September 27th 1944

Last night we slept in a small factory. There were plenty of sacks to lay on and we put sacks of corn all around us.

Jerry had just left that morning. The papers are talking of victory. They seem to think the war is over, but we have a way to go, as Germany won't give in yet.

We have not heard anything about our Captain. He has just disappeared. He was one of the best men I've ever met in the army.

Jim XXX

*Major W.G.C. Shebbeare was killed on the Caen Plain on July 18th 1944.

Holland

October 4th 1944

Dearest Nellie,
Yesterday we had the 'passion truck' to take us into the town of Helmond. It is a lovely town about the size of Winchester. I went into a café where there was music and singing. It was a posh place with waiters in black evening dress to serve you. The band even played some English tunes. Only one thing was missing and that was you, dear.
Jim   XXX
B.O.L.T.O.P.

Eastleigh

October 6th 1944

Dear Jim,
We all went to visit Bill on Wednesday, in hospital. His wound has opened up again so he has to stay in. Bill's new girlfriend, Margaret Carter, is going to visit him tomorrow. There is a fireman in the next bed, a jokey fellow that Dad knows. I bet they have some fun between them. They have nicknamed one of the nurses 'Sarge'!

October 9th 1944

Since you have been in Holland a while dearest, have you seen plenty of windmills? Have you had a nice welcome from the Dutch girls? I'm not jealous darling, but don't go falling in love with any of them, or else you will break my heart.

October 12th 1944

We are still free of sirens here, touch wood, but they have started on London again. I can't see you being home for your birthday or Christmas.
Nellie   XXX

Holland

October 12th 1944

Dearest Nellie,
The people here are rather funny. In some places they give us a welcome, in others they hardly look at us. The girls here are not so good-looking as in Belgium or France. They don't all wear clogs, only when they are working in the fields. They seem so clumsy, but they keep your feet dry and last for years!

October 14th 1944

I have only seen about four windmills. There are plenty of canals, which are a great nuisance to the fighting.
I have never told you this before but I also go to bed and dream about you at night. I lie in bed, thinking of home and what we are both missing. It nearly makes me cry to think of you, sweetheart. Let us hope our dreams of being together for good will soon come true.
Jim   XXX

Holland

October 23rd 1944

Dearest Nellie,

As you can see I have some different writing paper. One thing I can't find are envelopes. This paper came out of a Jerry Red Cross car, which was captured two days ago, with lots of prisoners.

I have just peeled the spuds for dinner. What I wouldn't give for a nice roast and a good dessert. I have already burnt the rice!

Jim   XXX

Eastleigh

October 23rd 1944

Dearest Jim,

Bill came out of hospital last Friday, but Bob has been taken away with Scarlet Fever! Mum is upset and hasn't had any dinner or tea today. He complained of a sore throat yesterday. The doctor came to see Bill and then had a look at Bob and at two o'clock he was taken off to Chandlers Ford.

Margaret, Bill's girl, came up to see him on Saturday. She stopped for tea, although she was worried about using our rations up. We coaxed her into stopping.

What would you like for your 21st birthday, dearest? Mum suggested a pair of gold cuff-links.

This is a little verse for you, darling.

My thoughts and prayers are with you dear,
And my love for you yearns,
With all my heart I wish for you,
Many happy returns.

Nellie   XXX

Holland

October 24th 1944

Dearest Nellie,

I will probably be spending my 21st birthday out here in the wilds. Maybe I will be home for your 21st, eh dear?

So poor old London is still getting the bombs. I thought they wouldn't get any more after we captured their bases. I wonder where they are coming from now? Most likely Norway.

It is funny that you never see Mum in the shop. I wish she would alter towards you, my beloved. It makes things rotten for you. I think it is jealousy that does it. But Dad is alright, isn't he? If Mum were like him, everything would be champion.

It must seem funny having a light on in the street. Won't it be nice when they all come back on again. Mum said the light on the corner of our road is lit now.

We killed a pig yesterday. We have had pork for breakfast, dinner and tea!

Jim   XXX

Eastleigh

October 26th 1944

Dearest Jim,

I can't get rid of this awful cold. Have you caught a cold yet, my darling? I hope not, or else you won't feel much like fighting, will you?

No letter from you this week, dearest. I am getting anxious. No doubt you are still moving on and the letters take longer to get here.

Mum took a parcel in for Bob, including his slippers. He is not allowed any visitors. Mum looked on the list at the Town Hall and it said his condition was satisfactory. The doctor thinks that Bob could be in hospital for three weeks.

Do you know Dulcie and Mary Crane, who live in your road? Well, they had a double wedding last Saturday. Their father had a job giving two away at once!

Nellie   XXX

B.O.L.T.O.P.

Holland

October 31st 1944

Dearest Nellie,

Well, this is my 21st birthday. What a place to spend it in! Twelve months ago we were all together at our engagement party! And the next day we went to Winchester to get the ring. Do you remember the siren went and we hurried down to the shelter together?

I miss you very much. It is ten months now since I have had any real leave. I had all those 'tip and run' leaves, when I used to pop up by cycle or train. Those are pleasant memories.

I was on guard duty this morning. After that I had a nice cup of tea with my rum ration, then some sausages and fried bread.

It is weeks since we have had a decent night's sleep here. I haven't undressed for bed for 23 nights now. What a treat it will be to get into a nice civvy bed, with sheets and pillow cases!

Jim   XXX

Eastleigh

November 5th 1944

Dearest Jim,

I heard on the wireless last night that Holland has had snow. Have you seen any, darling? If so, you will have the winter to fight as well as the enemy, and that's not going to be easy, is it dearest?

There are quite a few street lamps lit now, all over town. It is so much better than pitch darkness.

Bob is getting on alright. There are fourteen others in the isolation hospital. No doubt he has made a few friends. He has been in over a fortnight.

We still haven't a full staff at the shop. Joyce Raindall is away sick. Apparently she has boils in her eyes.

As I write this letter, both Mum and Bill are on their mouth organs. What a noise!

Nellie   XXX

Holland

November 12th 1944

Dearest Nellie,

I am staying in a farmhouse. There is an old couple, a young couple and four nice girls.

I was on guard duty again last night but never had to stand in a slit trench. It was two hours on and four hours off.

Jim XXX

*Slit trench- These short, rectangular trenches formed a linear defense system. These 'weapon pits' were dug along the edges of field boundaries.

Eastleigh

November 17th 1944

Dearest Jim,

Auntie May came to stay last night and we all went round the Meadowbank in the evening and quite enjoyed ourselves. Mum and Bill took their mouth organs. I think Auntie May enjoyed herself!

We have not had any more sirens, touch-wood. Auntie told us that London is getting these new rockets now. She has seen them go over and has felt the blast of one.

The street lamps are lit all over the place now, including our road. It makes one feel the war is over, except I haven't got you, my beloved.

Nellie XXX

B.O.L.T.O.P.

* The Meadowbank Public House was owned by Olympic Gold Medallist Tommy Green. It had a bowling alley and a gymnasium, where boxer Vince Hawkins trained.

*V2 Rockets: Long-range, ballistic missiles, launched by Nazi Germany from June 1944.

Holland

November 23rd 1944

Dearest Nellie,

I am now in another farmhouse with three other chaps. It is warm and cosy. The family have two little girls and one of them is called Nellie! They are bonny little kiddies.

The weather here is rotten. There is mud everywhere. No wonder the Dutch wear clogs. The rain has not stopped for two days and nights.

I have seen some of the lads from H.Q.F. Troop. This is the Troop that Ricky was in. They are collecting subs for his wife and baby. They have been left badly off since he was killed.

Jim   XXX

B.O.L.T.O.P.

Eastleigh
November 28th 1944

Dear Jim,
I do feel so sorry for Ricky's wife and family. Although I only met him once, it seemed as if I had known him for years. Have you heard anything about your Captain yet?
Nellie   XXX
B.O.L.T.O.P.

Deurne, Holland

November 28th 1944

Dear Nellie,
The girl of the house where we are staying wanted to write to you. It is in Dutch of course, but I have translated it as best as I can.

Translation:

Dear Nellie,
Your fiancé has told me I may write to you. He has been staying with us in Deurne and is a nice boy.
We have never had such a good soldier billeted with us. My sister Rika has a baby. The baby had a sore leg and he bandaged it and the baby is much better.
I hope you will see each other again soon,
Best wishes from my family,
Nolda Guort

Jim   XXX
P.S. I have plenty of Brylcreem, so please don't send any more just yet.

Eastleigh

December 9th 1944

Dearest Jim,

After tea tonight I visited the doctor, with my Impetigo complaint. It is improving I'm glad to say.

Auntie Fan had a Christmas present from her sister. It was a nice overall. She is lucky getting it without the coupons, isn't she?

In the newspaper it says that troops will be getting leave soon. It is such a long time ago that I saw you. What was the actual date you landed in France, dearest? Maybe you can't tell me.

We haven't had any more stray sirens. They tested it last Monday. We knew it was a test as they blew the 'all-clear' first.

Will you thank the girl for her letter to me, darling? She praises you up and I do feel proud of you.

London is still getting these V.2. rockets. Auntie Fan's sister had one nearby.

Nellie   XXX

Eastleigh

December 18th 1944

Dearest Jim,

I have filled in my Income Tax form today. I am allowed to earn £81 a year!

I went to the Regal yesterday afternoon and saw 'First of a Few'. It was sad. Leslie Howard was the star and he died in the end.

I do get fed up without you, Jim.

We have been playing dominoes. I have also started knitting a pair of gloves and a scarf out of an unpicked jumper.

Your sister Gladys is going to visit her boyfriend for Christmas. I do hope she enjoys herself. Although he is in hospital at present with a septic foot.

I wish you were home for Christmas. I have some mistletoe that wants hanging up and we could have some fun with that!

Nellie XXX
B.O.L.T.O.P.

Belgium

December 20th 1944

Dearest Nellie,
I'm miles away from my last place now, behind the line.
The baby's leg that I bandaged was very bad. It had started to go septic. It improved once he got the proper treatment.

Christmas Day 1944

I have sent a parcel off to you. It is a Christmas present. It is a set of undies. They are rose pink silk. The only thing is the knickers don't have any elastic! I hope you will be pleased with them.
We have had a simply lovely Christmas lunch, with lots of wine and beer too. They really know how to cook over here.
Wishing you a peaceful and merry Christmas.
Jim   XXX
B.O.L.T.O.P.

Eastleigh

December 27th 1944

Dearest Jim,

I'm sorry I have not replied sooner but as it was Christmas I intended on enjoying myself, and boy, did I!

On Christmas Eve we all went round the Meadowbank. I had the mistletoe on the go all evening! We came back after hours and pushed the tables back to make room for dancing. I didn't get to bed until 1.30!

I had so much to drink and finished up with a cocktail, but I never got drunk. I took your photo off the mantelpiece and we all had a toast to you.

I wonder if you will get your leave now that this fresh fighting has started in Belgium?

God bless you, Jim.

Merry Christmas!

Nellie   XXX

Eastleigh

January 5th 1945

Dearest Jim,

Did you say that elastic is in short supply over there, darling?

I'm beginning to think the same here. All the girls I know are now having to pin their knickers up!

I heard that three Eastleigh boys who went over on D-Day, came home on leave on Monday. Let us hope that you won't be far behind.

This is the third Christmas you have been away from home, dearest. Let's hope we can be together for the next one.

Mum fell down some steps on Sunday night and hurt her back. She has bruised it badly. Auntie Fan has to rub liniment in, three times a day.

I have started Mrs Bashford's cardigan. I will be busy!

Nellie   XXX

B.O.L.T.O.P.

Eastleigh

January 16th 1945

(After 8 days of leave)

Dearest Jim,
I do hope you got back safely, darling. I was upset last night when I saw you off. I was really glad that I didn't break down at the station, but I know you were feeling it too. It was worse going back this time because you knew what you were going back to, I expect.

January 22nd 1945

I'm glad the sea was calm for you, going back over. I hope you didn't have sea-sickness. I know I felt love-sick when you left that night. Let's hope it won't be another six months before I see you again, dearest.

January 26th 1945

Cyril Chapman, our Manager's son, was killed on Boxing Day, in Burma. He was 22. Apparently he was killed by a landmine.
Nellie XXX
B.O.L.T.O.P.

Eastleigh

February 15th 1945

Dear Jim,
Gladys and I went to the pictures last night and saw 'This Happy Breed', a coloured film. It had my favourite film star, John Mills, in it. It was all about a London family between the years 1919 and 1939. We had to queue up for two hours for the 2nd house, but it was worth it.

Glad told me that her boyfriend John, doesn't write too often. He says that he hasn't any news to tell her. What would I do, dearest, if you were the same? Surely he could write a letter to say how he was, or tell her that he still loved her. What say you, darling?

Nellie   XXX

I.T.A.L.Y.

(I Trust And Love You)

Eastleigh

February 20th 1945

Dearest Jim,

I saw Mrs Brown and family on Sunday. Do you remember their dog, with the abscess? They have had the vet round. He said he could do no more for her and would have to put her to sleep. Well, the dog saved him the trouble and passed away, just before midnight on Saturday evening.

Last night Bill had his dynamo stolen off his bicycle at work. It's no joke having things pinched.

Hazel's mum collapsed in the street yesterday. She had a heart attack, so Hazel has to stay home and look after her for a while.

Twice this week Mum has lit the copper to do the washing and it refuses to burn. We haven't any coal left and are without a fire. Roll on the summer!

You remember Muriel Whitlock, across the road? She has had a baby boy and is not married. Mum says he is a sweet little thing, with eyes as blue as the sea. He was going to be adopted but she can't part with him now.

Nellie   XXX

Eastleigh

February 27th 1945

Dear Jim,
I have just had a piece of grapefruit, the first I have ever tasted. It was quite nice. Bill told me that there will soon be some bananas in Eastleigh. Shall I send you one over, sweetheart?

I was getting my hand in on Saturday night, with Muriel Whitlock's baby. He is a fortnight old and such a sweet little thing. Muriel is going to call him John. She said I could take him out in his pram.

March 5th 1945

Let me know if you like Ovaltine tablets. If so I shall send some out with the bottle of ink you requested.

Jerry planes are bombing London again. We shot down six of them on Saturday night. I hope all will be quiet for tomorrow as Mum and Auntie Fan are going up to London to see Auntie's sister.

Nellie   XXX

I.T.A.L.Y.

Belgium

March 9th 1945

Dear Nellie,

I have moved around again, sweetheart. Do not send any mail at present as I don't know when I will be back to my usual place.

The news is really good and the lads are getting on with the job. I don't think it will last much longer. Then I can get back to you forever.

Saturday night I went to a fair in the town square. You would have enjoyed yourself, dearest.

March 18th 1945

Don't send any Ovaltine tablets for me. They are too sickly.

I saw in the Eastleigh Weekly, that three German prisoners that escaped, have been caught.

Also, I saw Vince Hawkins has won another fight! He is doing well. I was at school with him.

Jim   XXX

*Vince Hawkins – Eastleigh-born British Middleweight Boxer who became British Champion in 1946.

Eastleigh

March 19th 1945

Dear Jim,
Those German prisoners that escaped last week got as far as Eastleigh Station. Three jumped from the train and hid in a goods wagon. They were found and sent back to the camp, thank goodness.

March 23rd 1945

Little Ruthie has got the measles. She will be home from school for a fortnight.
Hazel came round today and brought me a tea-strainer and six yards of elastic. Now I can put some in the knickers that you sent me!
Nellie   XXX

Belgium

March 27th 1945

Dearest Nellie,

I have been boating on the canals over here. There are rowing boats and canoes, which one can hire. There are miles of canals!

I have joined the Royal Engineers for a time. I don't know how long for. I am officially the Carpenter, so now I can wear the 'cross-axes' on my arm.

Brussels is a big place, full of life and music. I caught a tram into the city centre and went to the '21 Club'. There were about two thousand people dancing in the biggest dance hall I've ever seen.

Jim   XXX

Eastleigh

March 27th 1945

Dearest Jim,

Ruth got her birthday card safely. She is a little better but won't go back to school til after Easter now.

Well, I still haven't received your parcel, with the nightdresses in. It has been 7 weeks now since you posted them. I shall be so disappointed if I don't get them, Jim. I expect you will be wild.

Do you remember last Easter, darling? You hitch-hiked from Aldershot that night and nearly gave me a heart attack, surprising me like that!

Our street lamp is lit every night now. What a treat not having to walk home in complete darkness. It makes me think the war is nearly over.

On Sunday, Win and I went for a bike ride to Albrook. We turned by the 'Dog and Crook', then on near Fair Oak and passed Fisher's Pond and down Sandy Lane.

Nellie   XXX

Belgium

March 30th 1945

Dearest Nellie,

I've got a new job. It is just temporary, in the Regiment Police, whilst the chap has gone on leave.

I clocked off at 4 o'clock today and caught a tram into town and went to the U.S.A. Cinema. I saw a lovely coloured picture called 'Greenwich Village'. It was very posh with seats like armchairs.

I caught a tram to Waterloo yesterday. It is where the famous 'Battle of Waterloo' took place. It was marvelous. I was up on top of the monument and a yank took a couple of snaps of me. I gave him my address and he said he would post them on.

The shops are full of chocolates and Easter Eggs here. The ice-creams are lovely too but expensive.

The news is good and it won't be long until the actual fighting is over. Then I can come back to you for good and all the chaps can go back to their loved ones too.

Jim XXX

Eastleigh

March 31st 1945

Dearest Jim,
That film we both liked, 'Cover Girl', is on at Southampton this week. It does hold memories for us, doesn't it? Every time I hear 'Long Ago and Far Away', I think of the day we saw that film together. I heard it on the wireless today and thought of you directly.
Bob has caught the measles off Ruth now. Poor thing!
God Bless You,
Nellie   XXX

Belgium

April 1st 1945

Dear Nellie,

Tonight I went to the 'Montgomery Club'. This place is a home from home. It is a big mansion belonging to a duke. The canteen is posh with waitresses too.
I've just heard the marvelous news. We shall be in Berlin before long!
Jim   XXX

*Montgomery Club- Situated in Brussels in the grand Palais d'Egmont building. It had over 350 rooms, shower facilities, barbar shop, laundry service and a large canteen. It catered for 10,000 troops a day.

Eastleigh

April 4th 1945

Dear Jim,
Before I go any further sweetheart, I have some good news! I have the parcel with the nightdresses that you posted over 2 months ago! I am more than thrilled with them.

Last night I went for a walk with Hazel. We picked some primroses and violets up by Pebbly Path. We walked through the woods and out onto Oak Mount Road. Up on the hill we saw the German prison camp, all flood-lit.

Potatoes are in short supply here and rice too. We shall soon be starving if things get worse.

April 9th 1945

Auntie Fan went into Winchester this afternoon and brought back some potatoes and macaroni. Potatoes are so scarce here at the moment.
Nellie XXX
B.O.L.T.O.P.

Eastleigh

April 10th 1945

Dear Jim,

Mr Chapman took me off the counter today, in the shop. We have been short-staffed and Ri was in a right mood. She don't like me and I don't like her. She says I have too much mouth. I thought I'd better warn you, for the future! I may be small but I say what I'm thinking. There will be more sparks flying tomorrow, I expect.

Some of us girls had sixpence worth of ice-cream this morning, the first I've had in a year. It wasn't bad but you could taste the dried milk. Still, mustn't grumble in wartime, must we, sweetheart?

April 14th 1945

President Roosevelt has died. How sad. It would have been good if he could have lived to see peace again.

Mary Harris brought a banana into the shop yesterday. It was about 5 inches long. It was a real one! She kindly cut it into little slices and we all had a taste.

Nellie   XXX

Belgium

April 18th 1945

Dearest Nellie,
I received your parcel and all was OK, except for the toothpaste. It was squashed at the bottom!
I bet that banana did taste good. It was decent of the girl to share it with you all. I have forgotten what a banana even looks like!
I went to the cinema last night and saw 'Henry V'. I didn't care for it much. It was rather dry.
Jim   XXX
B.O.L.T.O.P.

Eastleigh

April 19th 1945

Dearest Jim,
Gladys told me that they have chickens at your house now. They started with twelve but six have died.
Tuesday night I went to the Co-op dance with Hazel and the girls from the shop. A marine came in and Hazel thought he was Ruby Ballard's brother. I saw him again yesterday afternoon in Fleming Park.

April 24th 1945

I am sending you another bottle of Brylcreem. The man who served me asked if I had any empty bottles to return. He said the used ones have to go back before the shop gets another supply in. Could you send the empties back to me, dearest? It is for the war effort!
With fondest love and kisses,
Nellie   XXX

Belgium

April 27th 1945

Dearest Nellie,

I feel a little bit browned off today, as I am on duty til midnight. I know I wouldn't be if I were with you, sweetheart.

The weather is so changeable here. In fact, I'm thinking of putting my pullover back on.

About the Brylcreem, sweetheart. I don't mind sending the bottle back.

Fondest love,

Jim   XXX

Eastleigh

May 3rd 1945

Dearest Jim,

As for you being browned off at times, you are not alone. I often feel fed up, darling. I long for the day when you come back to me.

The 'Cosmo Café' has moved to the other side of the road and a new photo shop has opened next to Misselbrook and Weston's. Also 'Regal Studios' is opening next to the cake shop.

I hope to have a 'poly-photo' enlarged of Christine, the baby I look after.

There was a May Queen Ball at the Town Hall on Tuesday night. Mayor George Wright chose Pat Morgan. She is 15 years old and won 3 guineas.

I have bought 6 stainless steel dessert knives and teaspoons for our happy home, my beloved.

Nellie   XXX

Eastleigh

May 5th 1945

Dearest Jim,

It is raining here but I don't mind, as the news is good! We are waiting for V.E. Day anytime now. When it happens all our shops will close for the day and all the next day too.

The Meadowbank has all it's flags flying. We still have our old coronation flags and they are going up too. I wish you were here to celebrate the great day with me, sweetheart.

We have been allocated half a dozen oranges this week. I would very much like to send you one darling, but they go bad so quickly.

Nellie XXX

Royal Engineers
Petrol Depot
B.L.A.

May 7th 1945

Dearest Nellie,

I am with another regiment at present, working at a railway depot.

Isn't the news wonderful? We knew before the wireless announced it. All the sirens went and the church bells rang out. Last night there were fireworks going off and singing and drinking. I only wish I were in England with you.

Jim   XXX

Belgium

May 11th 1945

Dearest Nellie,

I wish you could be out here with me, dear. It is simply marvelous! I have been to the fair and had a good time. I didn't get to bed until one o'clock!

There was a big victory parade with two marching bands. I simply lost count of the drinks that the locals bought us lads. The town went wild. All the street lamps are on, no blackouts. A day like today comes only once in a lifetime, but the real celebrations will be when the whole lot is over in Japan as well.

Jim   XXX

B.O.L.T.O.P.

Eastleigh

May 12th 1945

Dearest Jim,

It is grand news about the victory in Europe! The newspapers say they will start to demob by July. I shall be so pleased to see you home, darling.

Auntie Fan is going back to London as soon as there are some rooms going spare.

I had a glass of brown ale tonight in celebration and a glass of parsnip wine at your house. We heard Churchill at three o'clock, on the wireless, then the King at nine o'clock.

We went over to Fleming Park to watch the Victory Parade. Hazel and I cycled to Southampton to see all the boats decorated with flags and hooters blasting out! What a sight!

Nellie XXX

B.O.L.T.O.P.

Eastleigh

May 14th 1945

Dearest Jim,

Yesterday afternoon, Hazel and I went to Leigh Road to see the big parade. It was a lovely turn-out. Everyone paraded into the Rec and we joined in the Thanksgiving Service. The Home Guard Band played and we all marched along Romsey Road and up Market Street.

The children in our road are having a street party on Saturday. We will have a real big do when the Japs are finished off, and you are home for good, aye, my darling?

It's not really peace yet, when we are still losing lives out on the Burma Front.

We will rejoice when all the world is at peace.

Fondest love,

Nellie   XXX

Eastleigh

May 17th 1945

Dearest Jim,

The pubs were allowed to stay open until 11.30 last week and there were lots of drunken people staggering about.

There was a fight outside the Town Hall, between two of our policemen and some yanks, who had pushed in some windows.

Auntie Fan has decided to stay in London, but she has had some bad news. Her married daughter, May, has run away with a married man. Her husband, Ernie, is quite a bit older than her. He wants Auntie Fan to live with him and be his housekeeper.

It was Mum and Dad's wedding anniversary the other day, 22 years!

Can you imagine us when we have been married that long, darling?

Nellie   XXX

Eastleigh

May 24th 1945

Dearest Jim,

I miss you terribly. I wish I had spent V.E. Day with you, sweetheart. The song, 'I'm a little on the lonely side', is one of my favourites at the moment.

A circus is coming to town in June. I will try to go to that if I'm lucky.

Do you think you might have to stay over there as 'Army of Occupation', dearest? I'd rather that than you be sent to Burma. We shall just have to hope for the best.

I have been collecting things for our happy home. I bought two sandwich tins and a patty tin for baking.

I am glad that your Mum is a bit nicer towards me. I do hope it stays that way, for both our sakes.

Nellie   XXX

I.T.A.L.Y.

Belgium

May 27th 1945

Dearest Nellie,

It is nearly five months since I was last home, dearest.

I must send my congratulations to your parents for their wedding anniversary. I can't imagine us being married for all that time. Won't it be wonderful when we do get married? That will be the day, darling!

I hope you have received the snaps of me in the 'Monty Club' by now, dearest.

Jim   XXX

Eastleigh

May 28th 1945

Dearest Jim,

Thank-you for the photo of you and your mates, taken at the 'Montgomery Club', and the souvenir of Antwerp.

On Sunday, Hazel and I went to the pictures in the evening. We saw 'They Dare Not Love', starring George Brent and Martha Scott. It was a lovely film but it had Germans in it, which rather spoiled it.

Next week 'Pygmalion' is on here with Leslie Howard.

On Saturday night we all went round the Tennis Club in Twyford Road, for our street party. We had a lovely time dancing and there were fireworks too.

Nellie   XXX

Eastleigh

May 31st 1945

Dearest Jim,

Just think, D-Day was almost a year ago, darling! Now the war in Europe is over!

There are two weddings in June. Betty Elford, our Assistant Cashier, and Barbara Luckert, from Grocery. I will wear my new dress. Barbara had a Cablegram from her young man about a fortnight ago, telling her to put up 'the banns', as he would be home soon. He is a sailor and Barbara hasn't seen him for 19 months!

Did you hear about the Vince Hawkins fight, darling? He went 15 rounds but lost. I was disappointed for him. About 250 people went to see the fight, including the Mayor and Tommy Green. Last night I went to the 'welcome home' reception, at the Town Hall. Vince had a patch over his left eye. You ought to have seen the crowd and heard the cheering!

Nellie XXX

*Cablegram-A message sent by a Submarine telegraph cable.

Belgium

June 5th 1945

Dearest Nellie,
I am in the canteen, writing this letter. It is my day off today, for the anniversary of D-Day. All the troops get a day off.
I have just been for a walk around the town. I visited the zoo. It was about as big as Fleming Park. There is a big exhibition here of Allied and German weapons. There are tanks, planes and even a V.2. It is a great big thing, the first one I've seen. You wouldn't think it possible that it could fly through the air on it's own.

June 6th 1945

Monty is coming this morning. He will receive the 'Freedom of the City', and is to open the new '21 Club'.
It has a grand dance floor. My mate and I managed to sneak in for a look.
Jim   XXX

Eastleigh

June 7th 1945

Dearest Jim,

I'm going to Portsmouth on Sunday week, with Mrs Brown's son, David. Their lodger, the Spanish boy, Angel, is coming too. Don't get jealous now, darling! Betty, from the shop, is getting married this Saturday and is going to the Isle of Wight for her honeymoon. We have bought her a green, glass fruit bowl as a wedding present.

Do you remember our old Mayor, Mr West? The one who's wife died in a bombing raid? Well, he died last Saturday, in his sleep. And to think, I only saw him the night before!

You are lucky to say that you have seen a V.2. I have heard the bangs and felt the vibrations though. That is as near as I want to get!

Nellie   XXX

Eastleigh

June 15th 1945

Dearest Jim,
Do you have plenty of potatoes out there, sweetheart? It is a very serious problem here. We had our first potato-less dinner today! Some people have queued for hours for them. Reading in the papers it seems the shortage will continue for some time yet.

June 19th 1945

Mrs Brown, the boys and myself had a lovely tea, right on the beach at Portsmouth. We had an ice-cream too and then went over to the canoe lake. The queue for the boats was so long that we gave up waiting.
My arms and face got sunburned and you ought to have seen my nose! Back at the shop everyone pulled my leg about it, asking if I'd been on the razzle!
Nellie   XXX

Eastleigh

June 21st 1945

Dearest Jim,

Coming back through Portsmouth on the bus last week, I noticed that there was not one shop standing that hadn't been bombed. Portsmouth has had it's fair share of bombing in the last 6 years!

Bill and his mate came back from London, on the mail train on Sunday night. He saw Billy Cotton and his Band. He has three new records, including the song, 'Don't Fence Me In'. It is one of the hits of the day. Do you know it, darling?

Nellie   XXX

Belgium

June 21st 1945

Dearest Nellie,
The food shortages seem to be terrible lately. Maybe it's because we have to feed all these Germans now. I'd let them starve, the same as they did to others. They ought to be shot, the lot of them.

June 25th 1945

I have some very good news! The Leave Roster is up and I am down for July 16th! That is 3 weeks from today, so not long now, darling!
There is still plenty of work to be done here. Today I started on a big meat safe, for the cookhouse. It is 6 foot high!
I have met some of my old mates, who are down here giving demonstrations on tanks, in the exhibition I was telling you about.
Jim   XXX

Eastleigh

June 28th 1945

Dearest Jim,

You are due leave on July 16th? Oh boy! Just lead me to it. What say you, my beloved? The next three weeks will crawl to us, don't you think, sweetheart?

You will be pleased to hear that potatoes are getting more plentiful again. Mum got 6 lbs worth this morning, without queuing for them.

You have a new kitten at your house now. It is a sweet little thing, full of energy. I hope your great big feet don't tread on him when you get home.

July 3rd 1945

Do you remember July 3rd last year? It was the last time I saw you before you went over to the other side. It was a Sunday and it poured with rain. We went to a concert at the Regal. You have been in the army exactly 3 years now.

Nellie   XXX

Eastleigh

July 5th 1945

Dear Jim,

I am writing this letter all alone today. Win has gone gooseberry picking, Bill is at the pictures and Mum, Dad, Bob and Ruth have gone to Weymouth for the day.

Glad and I queued up to see 'Going My Way' last night. It was a full-house. Bing Crosby took the part of a priest. He sang some marvelous songs like 'Day After Forever' and 'Swinging On A Star'.

Nellie   XXX

B.O.L.T.O.P.

Belgium

July 8th 1945

Dearest Nellie,
Only 8 days to go til my leave!
I feel a little shaken up after I fell off a tram yesterday. My left arm is still a bit stiff. The tram went round a bend too fast. Some of the drivers here are very careless. I am ok but a little bruised.
I hope to go to the beach this afternoon. I hear it is lovely down there.
Jim   XXX
B.O.L.T.O.P.

Belgium

July 9th 1945

Dear Nellie,

The weather is simply wonderful again today. Did you see the eclipse of the sun this afternoon? It wasn't a total eclipse, only just over a half of the sun was covered by the moon.

Yesterday afternoon my mate and I set out for the beach. We caught a tram to the tunnel, which goes right under the river for a quarter of a mile. The pleasure beach cost 2 francs. There was a funfair, an outdoor pool, cafés and stalls. It was just like England before the war. We thoroughly enjoyed ourselves. We came back by pleasure steamer. There was just one thing missing and that was you, darling.

Jim   XXX

B.O.L.T.O.P.

Eastleigh

July 12th 1945

Dearest Jim,

I am still in the pink and awaiting your arrival! I hope you are well after falling off that tram. I want to see you whole, not in pieces. How I am longing to see you again. It has been such a long time.

I am not starting any new knitting til after your leave, sweetheart. You won't want to sit and watch me knit while on your precious leave, will you?

We saw the partial eclipse here and in the newspaper it said that there won't be another one until 1999. What a long time in the future!

I will close now, hoping to see you on Monday.

Keep smiling til then, darling.

God bless you,

Nellie XXX

B.O.L.T.O.P.

* Jim and Nellie finally reunited on July 16th 1945.

Notes

Wartime Acronyms :
B.O.L.T.O.P. - Better On Lips Than On Paper.
I.T.A.L.Y. - I Trust And Love You.
H.O.L.L.A.N.D. – Hope Our Love Lasts And Never Dies.
T.T.F.N. – TaTa For Now!
P.P.R.L.H.- Postman, Postman, Run Like Hell!

Nellie's Family:
Mr & Mrs Moger
Wyn
Bill
Bob
Little Ruthie
Uncle Jack
Auntie Fan

Jim's Family:
Mr & Mrs Reynolds
Gladys
Pamela
Ernie
Norman
Grannie

Nellie's workmates and staff at the Eastleigh Co-op
Mr. Chapman, Manager.
Eydy
Ri

Betty Elford
Barbara Luckert
Nellie's friends and neighbours : Hazel, Muriel Whitlock, Mrs Brown

Places in Eastleigh:
The Meadowbank Public House
Cosmo Café
Fleming Park
Hann's Dairy

Dedication

Jim and Nellie Reynolds were my parents. They met as teenagers, growing up in Eastleigh. Both of their fathers worked on the railways.

Dad worked on a delivery van and Mum was on his round. They started talking and the rest is history!

Dad was called up on July 2nd 1942 and reported to the General Service Corps at Bodmin. He did his basic training before moving around the country, including to Bridlington. This area was chosen for tank training, in preparation for D-Day, due to it's similarity in terrain to that of northern France.

Why Dad was chosen for the 23rd Hussars remains a mystery. He became part of 'B' Squadron, as a Driver/Gunner of a Sherman Firefly. This tank, with it's 17 pounder gun, was capable of taking out a German Tiger or Panza.

Once he landed at Arromanches, at Mulberry 'B' Harbour, he turned left. He defended Hill 112, Falaise Gap, Villiers Bocage, then into Holland. At Eindhoven he turned north, liberating Bergen-Belsen and finally on to Hamburg.

In 2001 I took my parents back to Hamburg. I was told a story about a lake that had frozen over one winter. The lads decided to test the thickness of the ice. They drove a Sherman over it and the test was a success!

Dad was finally demobbed on March 23rd 1947. He and Mum married on November 1st that same year. I didn't come along until 1962, their only child.

Dad passed away peacefully at home on March 24th 2010 aged 86. Mum passed away on October 22nd 2016, three weeks before her 92nd birthday. During the house clearance, I found these letters. I could never bring myself to read them. Now thanks to Cheryl, they can be shared and enjoyed by everyone.

I still have Dad's dress uniform. I wear this to the Goodwood Revival and Remembrance Day. It attracts quite a bit of attention. In 1943 it cost £5 and 15 shillings, which was three weeks' wages then!

These letters, over 700 of them, were written between 1942 and 1945. How they survived is a miracle, but here they are.

Neil Reynolds
2024

Jim and Nellie
60th Wedding Anniversary November 1st, 2007

Printed in Great Britain
by Amazon